MIXED-MEDIA GIRLS

with **Suzi Blu**

MIXED-MEDIA GIRLS

with *Suzi* Blu

Drawing, Painting, and
Fanciful Adornments
From Start to Finish

Quarry Books
100 Cummings Center, Suite 406L
Beverly, MA 01915

quarrybooks.com • craftside.typepad.com

© 2012 by Quarry Books
Text © 2012 Suzi Blu

First published in the United States of America in 2012 by
Quarry Books, a member of
Quayside Publishing Group
100 Cummings Center
Suite 406-L
Beverly, Massachusetts 01915-6101
Telephone: (978) 282-9590
Fax: (978) 283-2742
www.quarrybooks.com
Visit www.Craftside.Typepad.com for a behind-the-scenes peek at our crafty world!

10 9 8 7 6 5 4 3 2 1

ISBN: 978-1-59253-769-3

Digital edition published in 2012
eISBN: 978-1-61058-392-3

Library of Congress Cataloging-in-Publication Data is available.

Design: everlution design
Photography: Shelley Metcalf

Printed in China

CONTENTS

Introduction

I'm a girly girl at heart. I get giddy over bows and ruffles, romantic cloth, dresses, glitter, and a whole lotta pink. The more glitter and sparkle, the happier I feel. But pretty alone is not enough—I want dirty, stained, and broken, too. I want beauty flawed. The lovely heroine living in a disheveled world—this contrast is the style of painting I call Girly Grunge.

The distressed look has long been popular among mixed-media artists who create the illusion of age and weather by tearing, sanding, and crumbling the papers they use in layouts. In my Girly Grunge art, there is a pretty face but everything else looks like it has been left out in the rain, run over by a car, or hacked at with a pitchfork. Why? Because imperfection is better. Living in a culture where images are highly polished and perfect, we are engulfed by art made from the computer world, and it doesn't feel real. We long for things on which we can touch the texture.

For the uninitiated, *mixed media* is a term that means using more than one visual medium in a work of art. In the past, artists stuck to one art form until they reached mastery over it: painters painted (some in oil, some in watercolor), sculptors used clay, and never did they mix. Then, in 1912, Pablo Picasso added paper to his oil paintings and the art world changed forever.

Mixed media is exciting because it rejects the idea that art needs to be pure and follow tradition. Unlike classical artists, who follow rigid rules, our potential is endless. Mixed-media artists are opportunists, incorporating whatever is around us into our work. Sometimes we are successful, sometimes not, but we are on the cutting edge of what is happening at this very minute. New ground is being broken in kitchens and studios across the globe by artists inventing techniques and experimenting with everything from fine art supplies, junk mail, and scrapbook paraphernalia to rusted hardware found in the street. In this book, you'll discover that mixed media is very forgiving—even if you think you can't draw or make art, you can do this. But you won't succeed right away. Initially, you will make bad art, and that will be uncomfortable, but if you are dedicated to the process, I promise, you will get better. When I first started portraits and toiled over drawing a nose, a friend said, "You're not going to leave it like that, are you?" The nose was bulbous with nostrils flared out too far to the sides. I didn't know how to fix it, but I knew someday I'd be better. Luckily, I was fearful enough of a life without art that I ignored what she said and kept practicing.

Vincent Van Gogh drew terribly when he started, with awkward heads on awkward bodies, but he kept drawing and got better. When we are beginners, we only focus on the end result of the art we like and therefore do not see the steps that went into making it—the years of practice and countless bad starts. You weren't born knowing how to write. Go get a pencil and paper and write your name with your nondominant hand. It will look creepy and awkward and you'll say, "Suzi, I can do better than this." And I'll say, "Yes, I know you can!" It's the same with drawing a face. You must learn the steps. You must sit down and do it over and over again until, like writing your name in cursive, you develop the fine motor skills in your hands and will be able to do it without thinking. Practice on the kitchen table, in the break room at your job, on the bus, wherever.

Quit decorating your craft room with shabby banners spelling out your name. Make art. Practice. Read the chapter, then sit down and draw. Don't wait for perfect paper: cheap computer paper is fine because you will probably throw a lot of early sketches away. *This* makes you an artist. Not your studio.

I AM AN ARTIST! SUZI SAYS SO!

Yes...you. Little and meek, wanting so very badly to make beautiful paintings, you think, "Who am I to do this?" Listen, the reason I started teaching
beginners how to make faces is that I grew weary of all the cutout photos of
dead Victorian people that dominated the mixed-media world. There is a for-
mula to making my faces and if you follow it, you can do it, too. No mystique.
You don't have to wear black and smoke clove cigarettes. In fact, you won't
be any different than you are now because you'll know how to draw a face.
You'll just be happier with your art.

Allow yourself the time it takes to learn. Stop saying to yourself, "Oh, it
will take too long to make pretty girls the way I envision them in my head."
Saying this doesn't help you get closer to your goal.

From here on out, look at each art practice session as a learning experience
without judging the outcome. You can't get better if every quirky body is
considered a failure. When you are an apprentice, the art you make is not
a direct expression of yourself. Ease up on criticizing yourself and look at
your art objectively. Make art, then walk away. Do the dishes, eat a sand-
wich, paint on wood. Practice, don't take your mistakes as proof that you will
never succeed, and you will get better.

YOU ARE AN ARTIST!

And if you don't believe it yet, believe that I believe!

Stay inspired by collecting art from contemporary artists who move you. These are by Tascha Parkinson, who makes a living as a full-time artist.

WHAT DO I NEED MOST TO MAKE BEAUTIFUL PAINTINGS?

Patience, focus, and joy. *Patience* for the time it takes to practice the techniques and improve your skills, *focus* for not listening to self-doubt and critical voices (in your head and outside it) telling you that what you do is not good enough, and *joy* because at the end of the day what matters most is allowing yourself time to create. Paintings will disintegrate over time and everyone who knew your name will be long gone. In the big scheme of things, the fact that you were Michelangelo or little Plain Jane will not matter in the least. Don't let ego get in the way of the happiness you get from playing with art.

chapter 1
Getting Started

The seemingly endless array of techniques and mediums available to the mixed-media artist can be overwhelming, particularly if you are like me and buy everything but then don't know quite how or in what order to use it. So before I explain the supplies we will use, let's get acquainted with the process we'll use in this book.

Mixed media is all about layering, putting one medium over another but allowing the viewer to see some of what is underneath. Layering gives a painting depth, mystery, and complexity. Unlike a "straight" painting where there is a tree and a ground and a sun, layering adds design, changes colors, and creates a dreamlike depth. The more layers in a painting, the more complex the painting is and the harder it is to figure out. Viewers find work more interesting if they can't quickly understand how it was made. The longer a painting holds the viewers' gaze, the more memorable their experience. This is what makes mixed media so fascinating. There are no limits on the number of layers you can add to a painting and therefore there is unlimited potential for where it can end up!

Layering 101

There are three key techniques you need to learn for creating complex, multidimensional mixed-media works with depth.

1. Transparent versus opaque
2. Additive versus subtractive
3. Light over dark versus dark over light

TRANSPARENT VERSUS OPAQUE

The key to a complex mixed-media painting is transparency, using several subtle layers that allow viewers to wonder which elements were applied first, and which came later. Use transparent layers to create the illusion of depth.

To successfully layer, any material applied over another must be transparent enough to reveal what lies beneath. It doesn't matter which mediums or supplies you use; if your layers are opaque, you will end up with one layer: the top one. Learning how to balance contrasting layers is key to achieving three-dimensional paintings.

To create transparency in your paints, mix them with varying amounts of glazing medium or dilute them with water. Use opaque paints or inks where you want to maintain the fullness of the form—for example, when stenciling and stamping a design.

Adding a little glazing medium to your paint for each square changes the transparency.

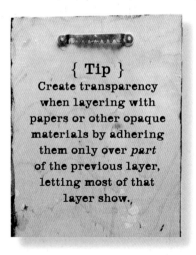

{ Tip }
Create transparency when layering with papers or other opaque materials by adhering them only over *part* of the previous layer, letting most of that layer show.

ADDITIVE VERSUS SUBTRACTIVE

Layers can be created with an additive or a subtractive technique. An additive technique is just what it sounds like: adding to what is already there. Spraying paint, stamping text, gluing down papers, and scribbling with a crayon are all examples of an additive process. The material used can be opaque or transparent, but it adds to what is already in your painting.

A subtractive technique removes something from your painting—removing color by spraying water over semi-dried paint and blotting it with a towel, for example. The subtractive technique makes that part of the painting more transparent. Carving into dried paint with a knife to reveal the layer underneath is another example of a subtractive process.

Additive process: a dark stencil is added over a white background.

Subtractive process: a wood-carving knife scraping away at the black stencil subtracts color from it and creates the next layer.

Left: Notice the difference between the opaque red heart and the many transparent layers behind it. How many layers can you count?

LIGHT OVER DARK VERSUS DARK OVER LIGHT

This is a method of alternating light and dark layers, combining both additive and subtractive techniques. For example, starting with a black background, paint a little light gray over it, and then overstamp the gray layer with a black text stamp. For the next layer, add transparent white. Go back and forth. Alternating light and dark makes it easy to lay down layers without having to think too much about what your next step will be.

Use white paint to stencil over a black background (light over dark), and then follow with a blue text stamp (dark over light).

My Process

When I discovered mixed media, I quickly realized it was no longer necessary for me to do a painting the traditional way. For me, it's not a lot of fun to paint a face straight onto canvas and be committed to sketching out the composition all at the same time. I prefer drawing a face in pencil on paper and adding glazes to it rather than painting it from scratch. It's easier to create detail with a sharp pencil than a flimsy brush, especially for beginners. Once the face is drawn and shaded with waxy colored pencils, I cut it out and glue it onto wood or canvas. Gluing down figures as I go gives me the ability to compose a more complex painting because I can tilt and place them at angles that would be hard to draw from the beginning. Through layering techniques, I build up my Grungy Girl's environment, adding texture, paint, and distressing methods, to give the painting that weathered look. Once I've added dimensional embellishments, I coat the painting with melted beeswax or self-leveling gel to seal all the papers and create a smooth, creamy finish.

Isn't

he

a

nice

surprise?

SPUNK

The best way would be

Supplies

Following is a list of the supplies I use in my process. In some cases, I specify particular brands of materials, such as Prismacolor brand colored pencils. These are recommended to achieve the look I am going for.

COLORED PENCILS

Prismacolor pencils are the only pencils you can use for my technique. They have the highest wax content of all colored pencils and are the easiest to blend into a porcelain finish. The high wax content also protects the paper from the hot beeswax when we add it to the painting at the end. (Paper not protected by the wax pencils will turn dark gray as the hot wax seeps into it.) You can work with other pencils—just omit the application of beeswax at the end.

GRAPHITE PENCIL AND KNEADED ERASER

If you're not already an expert at drawing portraits, you will need to practice, and a graphite pencil is the best tool for this. If you make a mistake, graphite is easily erased. I prefer mechanical pencils because they need no sharpening. Kneaded erasers are the best for getting rid of pencil lines without smearing.

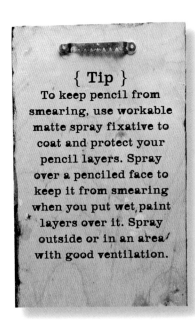

{ Tip }
To keep pencil from smearing, use workable matte spray fixative to coat and protect your pencil layers. Spray over a penciled face to keep it from smearing when you put wet paint layers over it. Spray outside or in an area with good ventilation.

WATER-SOLUBLE PENCILS

Water-soluble colored pencils, or watercolor pencils, are useful in mixed media. When wet, they bleed like paint, so scribbles and writing can be softened from harsh lines to watercolor splotches. For layering, you want a watercolor pencil that, when dry, will not come off when moisture is applied. Derwent's Inktense pencils' "lead" is actually ink-based. When blended with water, the Inktense pigment transforms into incredibly bright and transparent color that will dry permanent and will not bleed once dry.

MEDIUMS

Acrylic glazing medium. Use this for blending paint color and making it more transparent. Adding glaze to paint diminishes its opacity so it doesn't cover up previous layers.

Matte medium. I use this as an adhesive because it is fast-drying and nonsticky—you don't want sticky. Even when dry, sticky leaves a residue that is hard to draw over, and after all your hard work you don't want that on your faces. Stay away from cheap glues and use matte medium.

Texture mediums. Mediums such as fiber paste, molding paste, and glass bead gel add interesting textures to your creations. Fiber paste is thick with small stringy fibers in it and dries cloudy. Molding paste, which comes in light or heavy weight, is thicker than fiber paste and also dries slightly cloudy. Glass bead gel is lighter in consistency than the other two and has tiny beads in it. Bead gel dries clear.

PAINT

Acrylics. I like Golden Fluid Acrylics; they're perfect for mixed-media layering because they contain a high density of color. You can thin them down with water and the color remains strong. The color Titan Buff acts like an eraser for light-skinned complexions. Adding it to another color lightens that color to an antique tint.

Stewart Gill makes wonderful acrylic paints that are transparent and extremely creamy. The company's Alchemy line of interference paints is beautiful. Whirlwind is my favorite color. I use it for cheek and eye shadow color.

Gouache. This is a type of opaque watercolor. It is very opaque straight out of the tube and available in an array of beautiful colors. Opera from Holbein is the most fabulous color ever.

Water-soluble oil paints. These have vibrant depth and color, and, like oil-based paint, they take a long time to dry. Unlike traditional oil paint, they clean up with water. Use water-soluble oils over beeswax to take your painting further—rub it into grooves made into the wax for a distressed finished.

Watercolors. Watercolors create a nice wash straight on wood. Any brand is fine, even cheapie kids' watercolors. For intense bright colors, use the Dr. Ph. Martin brand. They come in a bottle with an eyedropper. Use straight or water down.

Pigments with mica. LuminArte makes many different paints, but my favorite product is called Polished Pigments Pure Color. These are pure color pigments mixed with mica to create a luminous powder that, when mixed with a binder such as gum arabic, becomes a permanent paint. I use Polished Pigments for a final layer of eye color to make it pop and as a glaze for creating layers. You *must* add gum arabic to the paint for the paint to be permanent. If you apply mica powders with water or other mediums, the powder will blow off once it's dry. A little bit of gum arabic goes a long way. Mix up just what you will use on your palette.

Fabric paints. Jacquard's Lumiere paints are the best for painting girls on fabric, because they are specifically made for fabric and, unlike other fabric paints, remain flexible when dry. Nothing feels worse than a rough painted shirt next to your body! Jacquard's Neopaque is excellent for covering jeans. Get Jacquard's medium to go with it, to make it blend easily. Jacquard also has fabric marker pens in flesh tones. Making girls on fabric is where mixed media is going next.

{ Tip }
Oil paint is the only paint that can be applied over beeswax. I use water-soluble oil paints and Shiva Paintstiks (see right) for this. Acrylic paints cannot be applied over beeswax because they are made of polymer and will eventually flake off.

ADDITIONAL DRAWING MEDIA

Chalk pastels. Non-Smear Pastels from the Stencil Collection are amazing for journal pages. Use them with a stencil brush over stencils. You'll need to spray your chalk works with workable fixative so you can paint over them.

Oil pastels. If you want to practice shading faces in oil pastels, use good ones. Cheap pastels are very hard to blend and in this case you get what you pay for. The best are from Sennelier; they are creamy like butter. I also use Shiva Paintstiks. I rub them into lines made in the beeswax layer and wipe with a towel to give my paintings a distressed look.

Although oil pastels are harder to use than colored pencils, and are not part of my process in this book, try adding them to the face after the beeswax cools. Apply white to highlight areas and blend out with your finger.

Water-soluble oil pastels. I use Portfolio Series from Crayola. I apply them sparingly, then wet them until they dissolve entirely into paint. These are great for journal pages. You may need to spray workable fixative on top if you want to layer over them.

INKS

Dye inks. My favorite dye inks are Tim Holtz Distress Reinkers. I love these fade-resistant and water-based dye inks in subtle pastel colors. Milled Lavender is my favorite shade. I use it on the face under the eyes for shadows.

Alcohol inks. I drip these straight from the bottle onto a canvas painting and dab with a towel. They add bold and brilliant color and make interesting designs when alcohol ink blender liquid is dripped over them. These inks dry fast, especially when used on porous surfaces, so work quickly!

GLITTER

I use glass glitter, which, as the name suggests, has glass in it. It's super shiny and dazzling. Cheap glitter looks cheap, and you want the best-looking things in your paintings. Martha Stewart glitters are also very nice because they are very fine and powdery. Pour them into vintage glass saltshakers and keep them on display.

FANCIFUL ADORNMENTS

Sequins, beads, tiny baby doll heads, mica chips, gold leaf, and whatever small shiny things are rolling around in your junk drawers are all potential decorative items for your mixed-media painting. Sprinkle objects around your painting to see where they might go, then glue down. To adhere larger embellishments, drop items into hot beeswax. I do this for most three-dimensional materials.

{ Tip }
To use smeary, sticky things, such as oil pastels, as a bottom layer, spray workable fixative first, then paint over.

SPRAYS

Use sprays over stencils or apply them directly to your work (dab with a towel or spritz with clean water to create interesting drips and light patches). Sprays such as Radiant Rain Shimmering Mist from LuminArte, Tattered Angels Glimmer Mist, and Tim Holtz Adirondack Color Wash from Ranger are all beautiful to experiment with. Or make your own spray with paint or ink mixed with water.

BRUSHES

Have a variety of brushes on hand, and use the right one for the job. Painting on wood surfaces can be hard on brushes, so don't buy expensive ones that will be used directly on wood. For painting on paper and smooth substrates, the best brushes are sable. The brush you want for eyes and lips is called a spotter. Have a few square and angled brushes in different sizes on hand for the cheeks and for under the eyes.

Things to Do with a Brush

Splatter. Load the brush with lots of watered-down paint, then tap repeatedly with another brush over the painting to create dots.

Dry-brush. To dry-brush, dip a dry paintbrush lightly into your paint, then wipe off most of the paint. Do not use water. Since the brush is dry, the paint will not spread like it does when applied with a wet brush. This technique is commonly used for stenciling. When stenciling, lightly dip a dry stencil brush into paint and make a circular, dabbing motion over the stencil for best results. You can also dry-brush straight onto a painting. The effect is very light and transparent. Dry-brush over dried molding paste to add color to peaks.

PALETTE KNIFE

Use a palette knife to load paint onto your palette and apply paint and mediums. I use one for everything: mixing color on a palette, adding paste to a painting, and as a tool for etching designs into wet paint. Wipe clean with a towel when you are finished and you won't need more than one.

SUBSTRATES

Paper. For all the faces in this book, I used cheap computer paper because it's thin and smooth. The thinner the paper, the better it integrates into the painting. You want the face to look like it's been painted, not glued, on the canvas after it is waxed. Faces and figures painted on thick drawing paper or watercolor paper will stick out from your substrate. Your goal is a painting that is smooth and flat. The smoothness of the paper also makes it easy to shade—the Prismacolor pencils just glide over it.

My favorite paper for art journaling is Arches Hot Press Watercolor 140 lb. It is creamier than Fabriano, which is also a good paper, but I prefer Arches for journals. I do not use watercolor paper for drawing faces.

Wood. I prefer using wood as a base because it holds up to the harshest of distressing tools. I get craft plywood already cut to size from art stores. Although I want to be a girl who cuts her own wood, I am a bit klutzy and afraid of sharp things, so that may not happen. If you have the tools and skills, cut your own.

Canvas. Although I was taught how to stretch my own canvas, stretching your own isn't much cheaper than buying it already stretched, so that's what I do. Get canvas that's been pre-gessoed so you have less preparatory work to do. Try different sizes—small, narrow, fat, and square.

FINISHING

Beeswax. My preferred method for finishing a mixed-media painting is to apply melted natural beeswax over the surface and let it cool. Because the collaged elements—the paper faces and figures, fur babies, boats, castles, and whatever else I've drawn onto paper—are glued onto the substrate, there is an edge around the paper borders that is noticeable. When you put hot wax over the glued elements, they become one with the substrate. A dreamy, thick layer builds up on top of them and levels everything out. Thus, it's nearly impossible to tell the painting was not entirely painted in one shot and is actually pieced together with glued-down elements.

An even more fantastic reason to finish with beeswax is the dreamy look it gives your paintings. Mediocre paintings turn mystical with beeswax! And it smells yummy, like honey. I buy natural beeswax in a bar in the candle-making section of my art store. To apply, I touch the bar to a hot quilting iron and let the wax drip onto the painting. I then use the iron to slowly press out the wax until it is smooth. You could heat up your wax first in a melting pot and brush it on, but you will still need to smooth out the wax with a small quilting iron.

You can also use colored wax on your paintings, but I recommend using only the nontoxic kinds. Many encaustic waxes contain damar resin, which is toxic when overheated. Kandi Corp makes an earth-friendly wax.

Self-leveling gel. This is an alternative to beeswax for finishing a painting and making collage papers unite with the substrate. Apply with a palette knife in long strokes and let dry overnight lying flat. It creates a lovely glasslike finish. I used it on both the Mermaid and the Fairy painting.

Using a palette knife to spread texture medium.

chapter 2

How to Draw and Shade a Pretty Face and Folk Art Body

For my style of painting, the pretty face is the thing that captures the viewers' attention. That is why we'll spend a lot of time drawing and shading the face—practicing until we can do it with confidence. The body, however, is simple, like folk art, so we'll spend less time working on that.

Drawing and Shading a Pretty Face

There is no shame in being attracted to a pretty face. We are biologically programmed to prefer balanced features over unbalanced ones because symmetry is a signal of health, a tool our brains use to ensure the success of offspring. To humans, beauty is found in a face where all features are in proportion and each side of the face is the same. If you struggle with drawing pretty girls, the trick you have been looking for is symmetry.

ens jouer avec moi;
as, j'ai dans mon panier
ne friandise.

I, que tu r
l aux anim
ont pas d'a

a. 1. s
ron of the op
gra fication.

«Minet, Minet, disait L

IT'S ALL ABOUT SYMMETRY!

If you were to draw a line down the center of a face, everything that is on the left must also be on the right. Not just on the opposite side, but in the same exact place on that side. If you want to make faces that are pretty, each feature must fall into the same line. The wonderful thing about symmetry is that if you have a ruler and a bit of time, you are guaranteed to master the technique of drawing a pretty face.

Before we begin, however, think about what is not pretty: features that are weird, distorted, out of proportion, one eye bigger or smaller than the other, lips that are crooked. Even though we aren't drawing realistically, most people don't look like that, and if they do, we generally do not consider it attractive.

A face that is not in line appears weird and creepy.

I didn't know there was going to be math on this exam.

SIZE MATTERS

You won't always have to line up a grid to draw a portrait, but if you do, especially if you are a beginning artist, you are more likely to get even results. Even though I've drawn girls for many years, I still pencil in a few grid lines to make sure features line up because nothing is more aggravating than spending hours shading and painting a face only to realize the features were not placed correctly to begin with. If you take care at the foundation stage, then the rest of your painting will come together more easily. Lining up the features is the hardest part, but get through this and then you can play. I won't tell you an eye needs to be a specific size because it depends on what size substrate you are using. For practicing, use paper that has grid lines already on it and measure your features with the grid boxes.

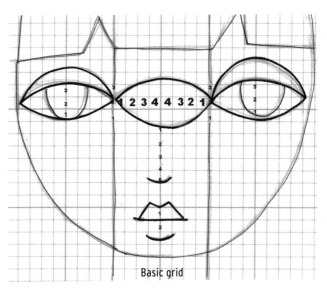

Basic grid

Talent, or something you can learn? A pretty face is guaranteed if each of the figures matches up perfectly.

START WITH THE EYES

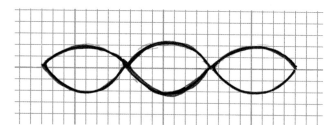

1. The easiest way to achieve balanced placement of the eyes is to first draw a fake eye in the middle. Draw one eye in the center, then make two eyes on either side of it that are the same size. Here, the middle eye size is eight squares across and the left and right eyes are also eight squares across. Keep all eyes the same size; this will help later when you are not practicing on graph paper and do not have a grid to cheat with. Leave a little room on the side of each eye to draw the contour of the cheek in later.

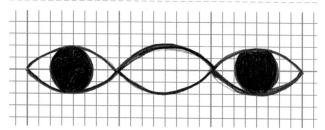

2. Put the iris into each eye. **Note:** The iris must be a perfect circle. Look into a mirror at your own eyes. The irises are always, always round. Always. Never are they lopsided or oval. Use a circle template to help you draw the circles. The iris needs to be in the same place on both eyes for the gaze to look natural. If the eyes are looking to the right, both irises need to be to the right. If your eyes look "off" or "googly," it is often because the irises do not match. The circle that you draw needs to be in exactly the same place in each eye. Practice on the grid paper and count the squares in each circle. This may seem tedious at first, but if you take the time to make well-placed, well-rounded eyes, the rest of the face lines up easily. A lopsided mouth or a too-small nose doesn't matter nearly as much as perfect eyes. So make that your goal.

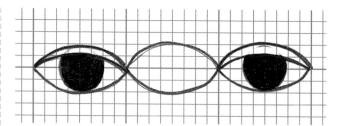

3. Leaving a full circle in the middle of the eye will make your girl look frightened or surprised. To achieve a relaxed eye, the upper lid needs to come down and cover the top part of the eye. Erase the top of the circle that will be hidden underneath the eyelid. **Note:** The more the top lid covers the iris, the more sleepy and relaxed the eyes appear.

The top of the circle will be underneath the upper lid.

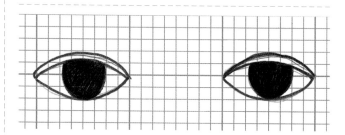

4. Erase the fake eye in the middle and you have a natural gaze.

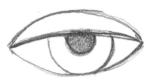

5. Now, draw in the pupils. Like the irises, the pupils also need to be completely round (a circle template will help you), and they need to be placed directly in the center of the iris. The more relaxed the eye, the more pupil is hidden under the top lid.

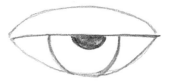

Fill in the dotted line and erase the pencil lines inside the upper lid for perfect pupil placement.

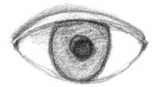

The lower the upper lid is, the more sleepy/sexy the eye looks.

A small pupil means the person is extremely excited or afraid.

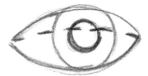

A large pupil means the person is interested in something and in a good mood.

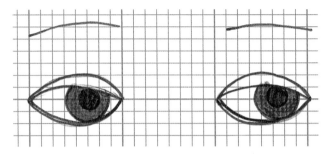

Regardless of which way the eyes are looking, the pupils stay in the center of the irises. For example, when eyes look right, pupils stay in the middle of the iris.

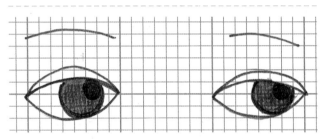

Pupils too much to the right and not in the middle look unnatural.

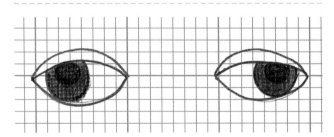

Googly eyes!

PLACING THE NOSE

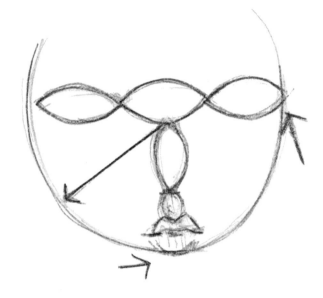

The nose is roughly the length of one eye. When practicing with grid paper, count how many boxes you used for the eyes, turn the paper sideways, and draw an eye vertically from the center of the fake eye (see photo, at right). Place the nose so that it sits at the bottom of the vertical eye. Placing the nose correctly is important because it is hard to fix after it is shaded. Alternatively, you can place the nose slightly above the bottom line of the vertical eye. The closer the nose is to the eyes, the younger the face will appear.

Who are you calling googly?

Place nose near the bottom the vertical eye.

Basic nose shape.

BASIC NOSE SHAPE

For what I call my "Petite Doll," a simple folk art girl, I use only a line to represent the nose, which when combined with well-placed, detailed eyes, looks just fine, but sometimes you want a little more realism. This is the completed nose shape (without shading) that I use for my faces. Practice drawing the nose until you get it right. Using a grid makes it easier. The ball of the nose needs to be centered in the middle of the line so that each side of the nose is the same on each side of the line.

PLACING THE LIPS

In my basic grid example in the right column on page 35, the lips are two squares down from the bottom of the nose, roughly one-fourth the length of an eye. Lips that are too close or too far away from the nose can make a beautiful drawing seem ugly. It is important that the nose and mouth be placed on an imaginary vertical line in the center of the face. Like a nose or mouth that is placed too far away from the eyes, a nose and/or mouth that is not dead center makes the face look peculiar. Our goal is pretty! Once you have the lips and nose placed, round off the cheeks and draw the rest of the head.

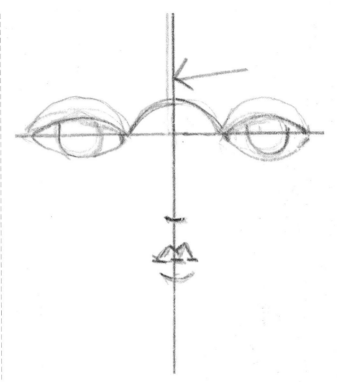

Lips and nose that fall on the center line are the foundation of a pretty face.

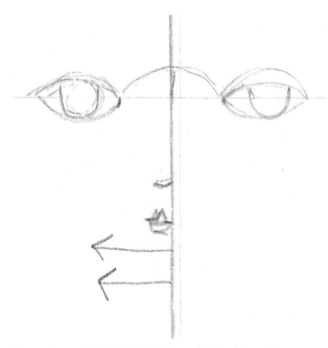

Lips and nose placed to the left of the center line make pretty eyes seem off balance.

SHADING THE FEATURES

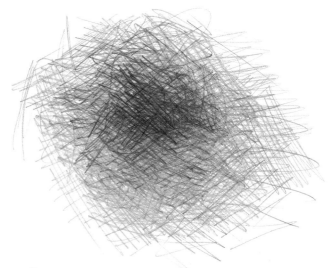

After you have practiced drawing the features, it is time to shade them. My faces are lightly shaded—I'm not fooling anyone that they are realistic. They aren't, and it doesn't matter. Subtle shading under the features is enough to make a pretty face. If you are making a Petite Doll (folk art simplistic girl), the shading is in the exact same places as they are for a more stylized portrait, except that with the portrait there is a more serious nose. Think of each feature and know that it must be darker underneath it to make it stand out.

The essence of shading is to turn a flat image into a seemingly three-dimensional one. This is achieved through the buildup of lines, or crosshatching, which eventually makes an area darker. Rather than pressing harder with your pencil to achieve a darker shade, simply continue to crosshatch over the same area, using a light touch, until the area is as dark as you want it to be.

Value

"Value" is a measure of the lightness or darkness of an object. Gradation of values is what makes up shading, and, to create the illusion of depth and dimension, faces need to have more than one value. Whether you are working with a colored pencil or gray graphite, your goal is progressive steps that slowly darken an area. Practice drawing lines on top of each other and notice how many shades of value you can create.

THE SPHERE

Stay with me! This diagram may seem intimidating, but if we break it down into its components, it's easy to understand. For an object to appear three-dimensional, it needs shadows and highlights. In the sphere diagram (right), the light is coming from the top left. Where the "light" strikes the sphere is the highlight, the lightest value. Shadows are formed when the light is blocked. Where the least amount of light falls is the darkest value—in this case, directly underneath the sphere. In between are gradations of value.

The Value Scale

If you think of a gradation from 1 to 10, with 1 being white and 10 being black, the highlight is 1 and the darkest dark is 10. Between 1 and 10 are the gradations of value (of gray, in the case of our sphere) that go from white (value 1), to light gray (value 2), to medium gray (value 4), to dark gray (value 7), all the way to black (value 10). Subtle shifts in darkness give a shape three-dimensional form.

Shading Tips

To make an object (or feature) appear three-dimensional, place the darkest value directly underneath it: under the upper eyelid, under the lower eyelid, and under the nose. These are the shadows, where the light is blocked by the object above.

Subtle gradations of value, like steps on a ladder, turn an object from flat and two-dimensional to three-dimensional.

ASSIGNMENT:
Shade a Sphere

Practicing spheres may not seem like fun, but it will help you immensely when you shade your portrait. Copy the diagram several times. The closer you get to subtle shifts in gray tones, from light to dark, the easier it will be for you to shade a face. It will be like chocolate cake. Cake, I tell you!

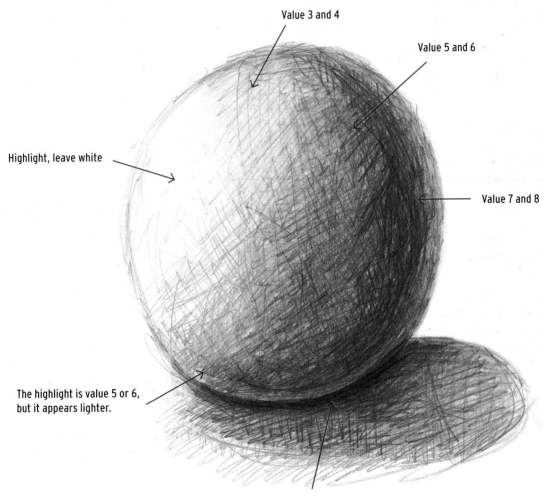

Value 3 and 4

Value 5 and 6

Highlight, leave white

Value 7 and 8

The highlight is value 5 or 6, but it appears lighter.

Your darkest value will be just underneath the object. This gives the illusion of depth.

SHADING THE EYE

For shading, think *eyeshadow*, not eyeliner. Many beginners press so hard around the eyes that what is supposed to be a soft shadow looks like Cleopatra eyeliner, whether they want it to or not. The most important rule to follow in all shading is to keep a light hand. If you think you are pressing lightly, press even lighter. Yes, it takes more time to see results, but you will like what you see. Areas to shade in the eye are under the top lid, under the lower lid, and in the crease. Press lightly, staying in one area, drink tea with your other hand (switch hands if one gets tired), and the result will be subtle shading.

1. Make the eye and cut off the top of it as instructed so it looks natural.

2. Shade in the iris.

3. Shade lightly under the upper eyelid and blend downward. Press lightly. Draw a crease in the upper eye area, and shade gently outward. The upper lid remains light.

4. Draw in the pupil and deepen the shadow that is cast by the eyelid. Hang out under the upper eyelid with your pencil, pressing lightly. The shadow will just happen. Shade the inside of the lower lid and blend upward. Shade the upper crease and blend outward to deepen it even more.

SHADING THE NOSE

Start building up the sphere at the end of the nose, just as you did in the sphere assignment. In this drawing, the highlight is at the top left, which suggests the light is hitting that part of the nose, so the shadow on the ball of the nose falls on the bottom left (in our sphere exercise it fell on the bottom right). We are implying subtle shading; light at the top of the ball and gradations of color below it, just like the sphere, is what you are creating. Take note of the white highlight that is directly under the ball, and how dark the area is under the nostril.

Copy this nose in your sketchbook. Practice it until you like what you see. I use this same nose over and over.

SHADING THE LIPS

For most paintings, I do not do much shading on the lips because it is a small area to work with. Save the details for when you are doing a larger portrait where you will have room for it. Trying to do this on a small face is not necessary.

1. This is the basic shape of the lip.

2. Shade from the outside of the lips in. Make it darker at the very bottom and keep it light in the fleshy parts of the lower lip.

3. Think of the bottom lip as having two spheres in it. This is where the muscles that make the lip protrude are. Although it is not necessary to have the lips fully developed, just a hint of spheres will give the lips a dimensional appearance. Once you have the lips and nose placed, round off the cheeks and draw the rest of the head.

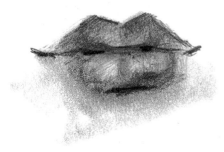

SHADING THE FACE WITH COLOR

Once you have practiced the basic facial features with graphite pencil and feel comfortable with drawing and shading the face, draw one on a piece of thin, smooth paper. This is the face we will cut out later. To shade the face, we will use Prismacolor colored pencils.

Using Colored Pencils

When you are first learning to use pencils, practice on paper that doesn't matter. Press lightly with any color. You may use any shade of color *except* blending white or cream. Press lightly with the pencil as you fill in. If you think you are pressing lightly, PRESS EVEN LIGHTER. Your goal is to leave no visible lines. Hold the pencil loosely, and build up shades slowly. Your aim is a gradual change in shade.

Once you're done with building up the shades, use cream and white. These are your blending colors. Press hard with these pencils to move the waxy colored pencil shades around. Notice how the white almost "erases" the color. Do not leave any areas of uncolored paper–even those that you want to leave white. The entire face needs to be protected from the beeswax finish with the wax from the colored pencil. Areas not protected by the waxy pencil will turn gray when the beeswax soaks into the paper.

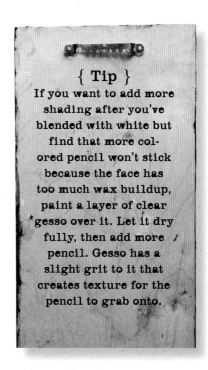

{ Tip }
If you want to add more shading after you've blended with white but find that more colored pencil won't stick because the face has too much wax buildup, paint a layer of clear gesso over it. Let it dry fully, then add more pencil. Gesso has a slight grit to it that creates texture for the pencil to grab onto.

BLENDING THE FACE WITH COLORED PENCILS

1. Using the cream pencil, sketch lightly under the eyes, in the upper crease, underneath the nose, and from the side of the right cheek inward. As with the graphite pencil, use light pressure. Cream is very light and you will barely see anything at all. That is good. Your goal is to build up shading slowly.

2. *In the same areas*, sketch lightly with light peach and then dark peach. Same areas! Under the eyes, under the nose, under the lips, from the side of the cheek inward.

3. Using burnt ochre, color the iris so it's darker on the outside edge than on the inside. Deepen the shadows under the eyes and in the upper crease. Darken the top lip and the side of the right cheek inward. Burnt umber is my go-to color for deep shading. It's dark enough to lay down real color yet light enough that it doesn't leave dark strokes.

4. Use rose around the eyes and on the cheeks and lips. Lightly!

5. Deepen the shadows under the eyes with dark brown or dark umber. It's okay if she looks tired, like she's been up all night. When we blend with cream and white, most of the shadows will disappear and only subtle darkness will remain.

7. To further lighten cheek areas or around the nose and forehead, blend with white. If you plan to finish your painting with beeswax, remember that you must color in white areas of the face, like the inner eyes and the forehead, with the white pencil to protect it.

6. Now we blend. Start with the cream pencil and press *hard* to blend all of the shadow colors together, avoiding the center of the face where the nose is. Concentrate on the area where the shadow colors meet the white of the rest of the face. Do not put the cream over the eyes or directly on top of the iris—just around the features, where the shading is. What you are doing is pushing the colored wax around the paper and blending it together. This is what creates the smooth, flawless finish.

8. With the face blended, some of the shadows might be lost. Put them back in with more colored pencil. Keep adding, using a light touch (with the shadow colors you used before), and blending (pushing hard, with white and cream), until it feels finished.

How to Draw a Folk Art Doll Body

A pretty head needs a pretty body, but it doesn't have to be realistic, complicated, or beyond what a beginning artist can do. I call this a "folk art" body because in traditional folk art styles, figures are often not realistically proportioned. These girls work better when they don't look real. Because folk art is typically created by nonprofessionals, it is considered a forgiving art form. The easiest body you can make is a geometric shape: a triangle torso with sticks for arms and legs. Simple! The face is pretty and the rest is as simple and whimsical as you like.

A body that is more complicated is really not complicated at all—just think of a doll. Each limb is jointed by a ball. You draw a simple limb shape until you get to a joint, then you draw the next part of the limb in a different direction. This is how you put the figure into different positions. Easy! Draw clothing over the limbs and you have what you will recreate on your painting.

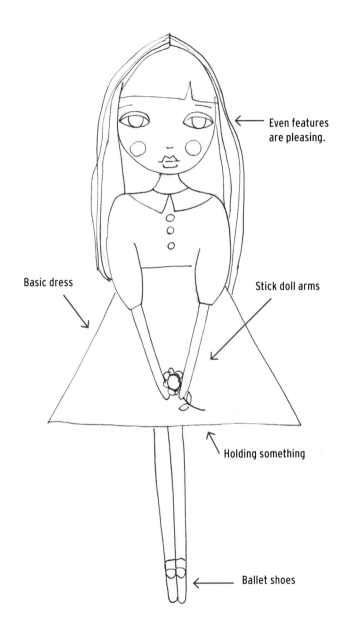

Even features
are pleasing.

Basic dress

Stick doll arms

Holding something

Ballet shoes

Don't these simple little shapes make you happy? If you make only these kinds of bodies, you will create many happy paintings.

Art dolls, like this one created by Brenda Figueroa, can be used as models to draw from. Make dolls, put them in different positions, and turn them into paintings.

DRESSING YOUR DOLL

Once you have a basic body that you are happy with, there are limitless options for the outfits you can design. There is a wealth of inspiration on the Internet to help you decide what styles and looks your girl will take on.

Keep an ongoing list of themes and costume ideas for your mixed-media girls in your journal. Themes can be personal or universal. Here are a few ideas to get you started:

- Gypsy, mermaid, angel, fairy godmother, tooth fairy, art fairy and other fairies, little girl, princess, ballerina, cheerleader, pirate, circus performer

- 1920s flapper girl, vintage beach girl, 1950s retro girl, girls from different cultures

- Rapunzel, Snow White, and other characters from fairy tales and Aesop's fables

- Figures from Greek mythology: Venus, Medusa, Athena

- Superheroes: Wonder Woman, Batgirl, Supergirl

- Iconic movie stars: Marilyn Monroe, Shirley Temple, Judy Garland

- Iconic movie characters: Scarlett O'Hara, Annie Oakley, the Little Mermaid, Pocahontas, characters from period movies such as *Dangerous Liaisons*

- Women from history: Jacqueline Kennedy Onassis, Joan of Arc, Queen Elizabeth, Frida Kahlo, Marie Antoinette

- Costume ideas: Mardi Gras, period dresses, Western, big flowery hats (Kentucky Derby), Halloween (kitty cat ears, puppy dog hats)

What other themes can you think of?

Mermaids are fun when they are whimsical.

Doodle swirls and hearts on clothes and wings to make them look whimsical.

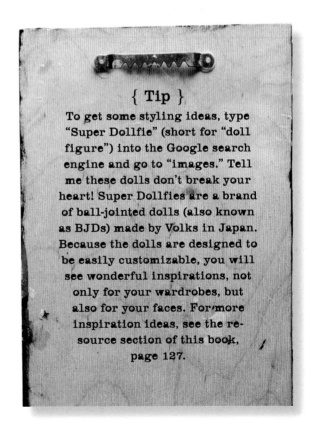

{ Tip }

To get some styling ideas, type "Super Dollfie" (short for "doll figure") into the Google search engine and go to "images." Tell me these dolls don't break your heart! Super Dollfies are a brand of ball-jointed dolls (also known as BJDs) made by Volks in Japan. Because the dolls are designed to be easily customizable, you will see wonderful inspirations, not only for your wardrobes, but also for your faces. For more inspiration ideas, see the resource section of this book, page 127.

DRAWING FUR BABIES

Let's face it, animals are more fun to have around than most people, so let's celebrate them in our paintings. Unlike girls, where we want the bodies to look somewhat proportional, the bodies of our animals need not be. In fact, the more quirky, misshapen, and unrealistic, the cuter they are. When drawing, remember what makes a child cute (large doe eyes, a stubby torso) and give the same characteristics to your fur babies; they will be cute, too.

This is my shih tzu, Finney Foo Foo. He's easy to draw.

Finney in color.

IDEAS FOR FUR BABIES:

✷ owls	✷ puppies
✷ sheep	✷ kitties
✷ fish	✷ ducks
✷ dolphins	✷ birds
✷ unicorns	✷ foxes
✷ lobsters	✷ wolves

(Okay, not all of these have fur!)

Large eyes and a big head = cute!

Scribble animals for practice in your sketchbook or journal.

EXTRA CREDIT

Search on the Internet for images of animals like dogs and cats and see if you can make simple shapes out of what you see. Kittens and bunnies are cute, but so are octopi. Practice making as many different simple cute animals as you can.

chapter 3
Putting It All Together

After all the practicing—all the drawing and shading, over and over—you're probably itching to do a completed painting. Your sketchbook is filled with ideas for girls and costumes and fur babies, you've pulled together your supplies, and now you're ready to play. Before you get ahead of yourself, let's do the first one together.

PROJECT 1
A Petit Doll: Your First Mixed-Media Girl!

This girl is centered in the painting, looking face-on, and the simple background allows her to be the focal point.

Objectives

- Using paint
- Creating a simple mixed media background

Materials

- graphite pencil and eraser
- Prismacolor pencils
- computer or thin drawing paper
- scissors
- 6" x 12" (15 x 30 cm) piece of wood for substrate
- matte medium
- paintbrushes
- Golden Fluid Acrylics in Titan Buff, Manganese Blue Hue, Pyrrole Red, Burnt Sienna, Carbon Black, Titanium White
- glazing medium
- rubber stamps and ink
- stencils and stencil brushes
- decorative papers
- rhinestones and jewels
- embossing powders
- beeswax
- quilting iron
- soft cloth for buffing

1. Following the steps in chapter 2, draw and shade a pretty face on smooth white paper. Cut it out and glue the face onto wood with matte medium. Draw the body directly onto the wood with graphite pencil. Yes, her head is bigger than her body, and, yes, that is all right. Big heads are cute; remember that.

Note: Once the face has been glued down, avoid using pencil on it for at least six hours—the paper might tear. Once the adhesive is completely dry, you can use colored pencils for details, but do not press as hard as you did prior to the head being glued down. Even when dry, paper is weakened once it has been wet.

2. While the face is drying, color the dress and hair with Prismacolor colored pencils in the palette colors of your choice. Write in words or draw designs. Although we will be adding paint, building up a first layer of colored pencil is a good way to test your composition before committing to saturated color. Even though any acrylic paint color can be "erased" by painting over it, starting out with colored pencil will give you a sense of what the finished painting will look like. You may think you want a black dress, but after it's colored in pencil, you may decide you would prefer red. Also, if you lay down a layer of colored pencil, you won't have to use as much paint.

I like to write words and phrases or designs as a first layer of the background. It might be completely covered with paint at the end, but it gives you a place to start, and sometimes it shows through slightly and adds depth and excitement. (It is also fun to write secret love letters in paintings, and then cover them up entirely with paint so no one but you knows they are there. It adds to the magic.)

the hair Burnt Sienna. If you want the hair to be opaque, you will need a few coats. A glaze (paint mixed with acrylic glazing medium) of Titan Buff on the face gives a smooth complexion and will erase any color mistakes. Lay it down with a brush but have a clean dry brush handy to wipe the excess away. Clean the dry brush by wiping it immediately with a towel, so it can be used again. Titan Buff smoothes out any leftover pencil lines. Don't go overboard with it—consider it just an overlay; you are not painting much on the face. Mix Manganese Blue with the Titan Buff and add glazing medium. Paint the center of the dress and around the edges of the eyes to separate the iris from the pupil and make them pop.

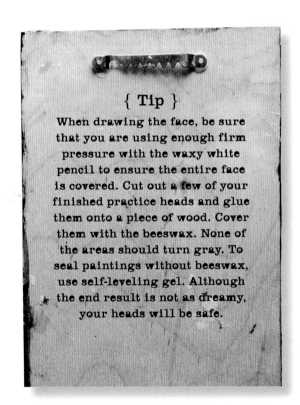

{ Tip }

When drawing the face, be sure that you are using enough firm pressure with the waxy white pencil to ensure the entire face is covered. Cut out a few of your finished practice heads and glue them onto a piece of wood. Cover them with the beeswax. None of the areas should turn gray. To seal paintings without beeswax, use self-leveling gel. Although the end result is not as dreamy, your heads will be safe.

3. Paint the dress and eyes blue straight from the bottle. Paint the arms, collar, and leggings white; use red for the lips and heart on the pocket. Paint the shoes black. Paint

4. Stamp and/or stencil designs onto both the background and the figure. If the dress is dark, stamp a light color on it. Alternatively, if the background is light, stencil a darker color over the top. Get some of the background color onto her dress and vice versa. This unifies the painting and makes it more complex and interesting than if her dress were solid and plain. Create a loose wash (paint mixed with water) and paint it around the figure, letting some of the wood show through.

5. Tear collage papers and adhere them sparingly and randomly to your piece with matte medium. Less is more, so show restraint. I know how pretty scrapbook papers can be, but putting too much into one painting can overwhelm the piece. Choose colors that match your palette and that have some pattern to them. Placing them diagonally from each other creates a balanced look.

6. This is the last stage of the painting before finishing with beeswax, so finish up any painting or stamping you think the painting might need, and add other three-dimensional items, such as rhinestones and jewels. Add embossing powders to raise a detail, such as on the heart.

7. Cover the painting with beeswax chips, avoiding your three-dimensional items, and smooth down the wax layer with the quilting iron.

{ Tip }

Want your painting to shine? If you buff the cooled beeswax with a soft cloth, it will polish the wax over your painting into a shiny top coat.

TO HANG

Attach a sawtooth hanger to the back of the piece with a hot glue gun. You can use this for both 6" x 12" (15 x 30 cm) and 12" x 24" (30 x 60 cm) thin craft plywood paintings.

If your wood is heavier than thin plywood, or if you would like a softer finish, drill holes into the top of the painting and hang from pretty ribbons.

PROJECT 2
Marie Antoinette: Making It Larger

Now that you know the basic process of making a mixed-media girl (or, as I like to call them, Petite Doll) painting, you will take your drawing and mixed-media skills further. In this project, we are using a larger substrate to create a larger-than-life Marie Antoinette figure and adding a textured background using molding paste.

In this painting, the figure is still the focal point, but this time you will imply a bit of background. Notice I say imply—when the figure is the focal point, you don't want anything else so prominent that it competes with her. But this can be difficult when you want to add other things to the painting. What I have learned is that objects such as trees, a castle, or a gazebo need only a general form and no detail. This gives the painting a background and a setting, but allows the girl to command our attention. Because Marie Antoinette takes up most of the composition space, you don't need to have a lot going on behind her.

Objectives
- Using molding paste
- Creating background elements
- Adding text
- Incorporating collage papers
- Using the dripping technique
- Adding wool to beeswax
- Adding three-dimensional accessories

Materials
- graphite pencil and eraser
- Prismacolor pencils
- computer or thin drawing paper
- scissors
- 12" x 24" (30 x 60 cm) piece of wood
- matte medium
- paintbrushes
- Golden Fluid Acrylics in Manganese Blue + Titan Buff (sky), Quinacridone Magenta + Titan Buff (dress), Green + Titan Buff (grass), Raw Umber (for glaze)
- molding paste
- palette knife
- wool roving
- glazing medium
- rubber stamps and StazOn permanent and dye-based inks
- stencils
- decorative papers
- vintage text paper
- brown ink
- paper towels
- black oil pastel
- embroidery floss
- beeswax
- quilting iron

PREPARATION
Make an Inspiration Page

I like to keep inspiration pages inside a loose-leaf note-book so I can take the pages out if I need to. Write or draw everything you are going to put into the painting: the color palette, the papers you think will work, the accessories and items. This helps immensely while you work on your painting and keeps you from blocks where you forget what you wanted to do.

Create an inspiration page with stick drawings, papers, and colors you want to use for your Marie Antoinette painting.

Research

The body structure of Marie Antoinette is very simple: a basic torso, a tiny waist, and a big fat skirt. Do an Internet search of "Marie Antoinette dress" to get some ideas. Another great resource is Dover Clip Art books. Also, you need to consider where in the composition you will place the figure. Do not make her pose too complicated. Keep it simple.

Experiment with composition. Here, I've drawn a girl looking in one direction and then in another. Notice that the figure is not in the center of the painting but off to one side, which is more interesting.

ACCESSORY IDEAS

Ideas for objects to go in your
Marie Antoinette painting:

✽ swan

✽ birdcage

✽ gazebo

✽ fancy tiered cake

✽ parasol

✽ castle

✽ little dogs

✽ bows and buttons

✽ Victorian flowers

✽ photos

THE PALETTE

Although including the right accessories is key to communicating your painting's theme to the viewer, the palette colors you choose will tell more. Using the wrong colors and the wrong shades is a common mistake that beginners make. Colors evoke mood, and if you paint Marie Antoinette in all red and black, the viewer might not understand who she is. Think about your color palette before you begin painting.

Marie Antoinette is associated with pastels, and any combination works: baby pinks and blues, pale yellows and light mint green, and lavender, bluish gray, and washed-out pumpkin (but using all the pastels together may look like a pastel circus). Add Titan Buff to your paint colors to give them a vintage feel.

Marie Antoinette is not only pastel. She is a queen and has the best of everything. To accent the pastel palette, use gold and bright pink. I like to call the accent pink Vivid Strawberry. It adds punch to the pastels and turns what is just shabby and pretty into high glamour, which is how Marie was. To me, bright pink is Marie Antoinette's spirit. Pink, not red, which is for an older, wiser woman. Marie Antoinette became a queen at a very young age, so pink is more playful and fitting. (Red, as you will see in a later project, works very well for mermaids and sirens, who are more seductive.) Hot pink is the juice among all the powdery colors. It is the "new" contrasting with the "old." Although I did not use it in this particular painting, try adding gold leaf.

{ Tip }

Pick up gold leaf with
a brush that has matte
medium on it and glue
down randomly.

Assignment: Sketch Marie Antoinette

Practice drawing Marie Antoinette dolls and accessories in your sketchbook.

MAKING MARIE ANTOINETTE

1. Following the steps in chapter 2, draw and shade the face on paper, cut out, and position the head on the wood. Glue down with matte medium. Draw the body, using your research sketches as a reference for the dress. Draw in a horizon line behind the figure and the shape of something in the distance, such as a tree, a gazebo, or a swan. I drew a simple castle that reminded me of Versailles. Paint the dress, ground, and sky with a wash of your palette colors. **Note:** In the previous project, we colored the first layer with colored pencils to try out our color choices before committing to them with paint. This is not always necessary. Sometimes just a wash—paint mixed with ample water—of color where you want it is enough to give you an idea.

2. Scrape molding paste around the head with a palette knife to imply hair. No need for individual strands. Your goal is texture. Let the molding paste dry for at least 6 hours. You can also embed wool roving into the wet molding paste to add even more texture to the hair. While molding paste dries, paint the eyes, lips, and cheeks with paint mixed with glazing medium.

3. When the molding paste is dry, stamp randomly onto the painting. I used a text stamp (a staple you will find in nearly all of my work) and a harlequin-patterned stamp. For stamping, use StazOn permanent inks as well as dye-based inks. Dye-based inks will smear when water is added to them, which adds to the drippy, shabby, left-in-the-rain effect. Alternate permanent stamping and smeary stamping for complex layers.

To unify the painting, truly be random with stamping. Close your eyes if you have to and stamp away, especially if you are using ink that is not permanent. If the result is horrible, you can quickly wipe it away. Your goal is to create a painting that is complex and thought-provoking, without giving the process away: "Oh, yes, see, here is where she stamped." Stamp onto the background and onto the figure. Even stamp a little on her face. Yes, her face. Also stamp onto the dry modeling paste in a few spots.

4. To give her dress texture and pattern, spread molding paste over a stencil with a palette knife, then lift the stencil. Repeat until you like the design. Let dry for a few hours before layering paint over the paste.

6. Use vintage text paper to cover the castle. It will look less like a castle when you are through, but that is acceptable. We are implying a castle, not painting a realistic one. Then quickly do the dripping technique: brush watered-down brown ink across the top of the painting and let it drip down. Blot away any drips you do not want with a paper towel. Glaze around the body with brown paint, smoothing outward to blend.

5. With matte medium, glue down decorative papers that match your theme. In the sky, put vintage blue scrap paper, and in the dress use bold pink papers. Rip the edges so they look organic, old, and torn.

7. Draw a simple birdcage in her hand with black oil pastel.

8. Glue strands of white, light blue, or pink embroidery floss into her hair with matte medium. Dab Titanium White on her hair. Paint a bird, then stamp and collage until you like it. Glue the bird on her head with hot beeswax. Wax the entire painting, but stay away from some of the hair where the molding paste peaks are very high. Smooth the wax with a quilting iron.

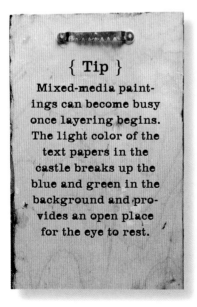

{ Tip }

Mixed-media paintings can become busy once layering begins. The light color of the text papers in the castle breaks up the blue and green in the background and provides an open place for the eye to rest.

COMPOSITION: THE SEVEN ELEMENTS OF DESIGN

Composition is the coming together of many parts: line, shape, texture, form, color, space, and value—the seven elements of design. Studying paintings you like, finding each of these elements, and understanding how they help create a good painting will help you become more successful in your own work.

Let's break down my Marie Antoinette painting as it relates to the seven elements of design.

Line. Although Marie is a simply drawn folk art figure, the simplest of lines can be interesting. Most of the lines are rounded and curved and her head is set at an angle. This is more interesting than the placement of our first painted girl, who stood stiffly in the middle. The lines that create Marie are gentle and flowing, suggesting to the viewer that Marie is a gentle and kind person. You can speak volumes with a line.

Shape. Lines curve and close and form shapes, and we can see that Marie is a shape. But notice the shapes the lines create in the negative areas around the figure. The more interesting the negative shapes are, the more complex the design.

Texture. Just by looking at the painting, we can feel the tactile surface. There are abstract flowers on her dress that feel bumpy, and her hair is a coarse, tangled mess. This contrasts with the smooth, almost watery, feeling of the grass and sky. This visible difference makes a painting complex.

Form. Form is similar to shape, but, in this case, I'll refer to the form the substrate takes—it is rectangular and narrow. If the painting were small and square, she wouldn't look as elegant.

Color. In this painting, color is all about contrasts: bright versus cool tones. The warmth of her dress color contrasts with the cool green and blue sky, which makes the figure stand out. If her dress were cool colors like the rest of the painting, Marie would fade into the background. Use spots of warm color amid cool colors to lead the viewer's eye to where you want it to go.

Space. When looking at art, viewers need space, somewhere for their eyes to rest. Although there are pattern, texture, and chaos in places, they are balanced with quiet places where not much is happening.

Value. The more variations in value, the more a painting will hold the viewer's attention. In mixed-media works, multiple layers of color in certain places will naturally deepen the value of those areas; create variation in value by keeping other places light.

BALANCE

This composition also works because it is balanced. Because the head is at the top left, something with weight was needed in the bottom right to balance the painting. The birdcage mimics the shape of Marie's head and is painted in black so that we see it. If the cage were white or smaller or in another corner, it would not have the necessary weight. To counter the heaviness of the black cage, I added the wooden bird above her head. I painted the bird the same blue as the paper flowers on the cage to further tie them together.

When adding elements to your painting, always step back and see how the painting would look if something were added to balance it.

PROJECT 3
The Gypsy Girl: Creating a Carnival Environment

Step right up, ladies and gentlemen, and gaze upon the greatest congregation of sights and thrills ever to be assembled under one roof! It's a Petite Carnival!

Everyone loves a carnival, especially mixed-media artists. It's bawdy, disheveled, and full of shady, fantastical delights. Perfect for the obsession with all things grungy and childlike.

Objectives
- Using wider substrate
- Creating a complex composition
- Using fabric
- Incorporating accessories (pets, objects, buildings)
- Creating intense layering
- Using heavy embedded objects

Materials
- graphite pencil and eraser
- Prismacolor pencils
- computer or thin drawing paper
- scissors
- 12" x 12" (30 x 30 cm) or larger canvas substrate
- matte medium
- paintbrushes
- spray bottle
- Golden Fluid Acrylics in Titan Buff, Titanium White, Manganese Blue Hue, Jenkins Green, Permanent Green Light, Yellow Ochre, Carbon Black, Quinacridone Magenta, Quinacridone Violet, Ultramarine Blue, Hansa Yellow Opaque, and Pyrrole Red
- paper towels
- brightly colored cloth
- decorative papers
- dried flowers, gold stars, birds
- stencils and stencil brushes
- glazing medium
- embroidery floss
- beeswax
- miniature wooden fence
- vintage jewelry and other embellishments
- vintage text paper
- small piece of scrap wood
- glue gun or E6000
- quilting iron

DESIGNING A SCENE

Until now, the figure has been the main focal point, and that has been easy. But when you add more elements to a painting, things can quickly go awry.

To begin a scene, you need a big enough substrate. This painting is on a large canvas. Although I prefer using wood as a base because it holds up to the harshest of distressing tools, canvas is easier to paint on. It is also available in different sizes.

The trick to maintaining a mixed-media style in an environment painting is controlled chaos. There are two distinct palettes going on here and never do they cross. Everything that is carnival is bright, opaque, and vivid. Everything that is landscape is dull, transparent, and neutral. This division keeps the scene harmonious and easy to understand. Beginners love color and get excited easily about purple and pink and soon everyone's hair is fluorescent lime and mountains and trees look more like a psychedelic nightmare than anything resembling real life. I am not inhibiting your creativity, and no, our goals do not include realism, but until you know how to balance bright colors, refrain from using them everywhere.

The gaudy circus colors work because they are tempered by the muted browns and greens. Also, the blank areas that are not circus colors give the viewer's eye a place to rest. Had I not divided my palette into natural/carnival, the landscape would be swallowed by color and the viewer would not know where to look first. Add bright color but keep the main background palette muted and your painting will make sense.

1. Sketch a scene. Keep it simple. Draw and color the girls' faces on paper. Cut it out and put aside. Glue down one or more of the main figures. I do this early on; if the face is glued down later over papers, it will look bumpy when it dries. Draw sketch lines to represent a simple landscape. Lay down a foundation layer of color with colored pencils and paint. You can change your colors at any time, but it's a good idea to get a general sense of what you want.

2. To create the earthy feeling of the grass and dirt, spray and drip paint over the foundation layer. Let the paint dry slightly, then dab at it with a paper towel to lift color. Continue making drips and sprays of color.

3. Add details, such as circus tents and houses. Glue patterned fabric and decorative paper over blocked areas of color to create your various elements. Glue down dried flowers and tiny stars.

4. Stencil over the grass and also over the sky, to help integrate the areas into the painting. The key to integration is adding a little of what is in one place to some place else. You want everything to be part of the same family. If you haven't done so already, add other figures to the canvas, making sure no collage papers are behind the faces to cause creases.

5. Mix 3 parts glazing medium to 1 part brown paint. Brush around each figure and blend out with a dry brush. This will create depth around the figures and separate them from the background.

7. Drip hot wax in areas and place larger objects into it to adhere. Large paper flowers, a miniature dollhouse fence, and wooden birds give the work a slight sculptural feel. Cover the entire painting.

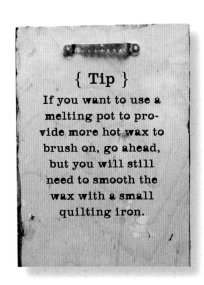

{ Tip }

If you want to use a melting pot to provide more hot wax to brush on, go ahead, but you will still need to smooth the wax with a small quilting iron.

6. Create hair by gluing on embroidery floss. Paint over the floss to help integrate it into the painting.

8. Add glitz by embedding jewelry pieces in the hot wax.

If a large scene is intimidating, create a smaller canvas first.

10. Wax the entire painting, and smooth the wax with a quilting iron.

9. Glue vintage text paper to a piece of scrap wood to create a midway sign. Press fabric into the hot wax. This gives the painting even more over-the-top drama. With a glue gun, adhere the sign to the back of the painting. If you live in a humid climate, use a stronger glue, such as E6000.

PROJECT 4
Angels and Fairies:
Adding Wings

For this project, we will paint portraits of a fairy and an angel. We will keep the figure the focal point and the background abstract, but we'll create a more stylized face. Unlike Marie Antoinette, who had a small folk art dash of a nose, these faces are more expressive.

I've combined two projects to show that the only difference between a fairy and an angel is the wings.

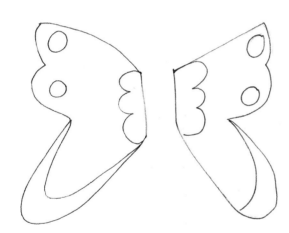

Fairy wings

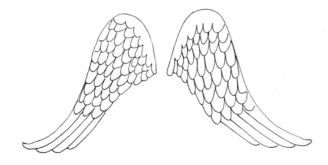

Angel wings

FAIRY PORTRAIT
Objectives
- Making stylized features
- Using fiber paste
- Incorporating natural materials

Materials
- graphite pencil and eraser
- Prismacolor pencils
- computer or thin drawing paper
- scissors
- 16" x 20" (40 x 50 cm) canvas or wood substrate (I used canvas)
- matte medium
- palette knife
- fiber pastemolding paste
- stencils
- spray bottle
- Radiant Rain spray in pink (or make your own)
- Tattered Angels Glimmer Mist Chalkboard (in Strawberry Shortcake)
- paper towels
- paintbrushes
- Golden Fluid Acrylics in Titanium White, Raw Umber, Quinacridone Magenta, Quinacridone Violet, and Pyrrole Red
- stencil brush
- flowers and other natural materials, such as small twigs or bits of dried leaves (don't go too crazy—you don't want the embellishments to trump the painting; with three-dimensional items, less is always more)
- Polished Pigments mixed with gum arabic in color of your choice (for eye color)
- glitter
- tiny beads and sequins
- beeswax
- quilting iron

Gather colors and materials onto a page to compose the palette of your painting before you begin.

Optional extras:
- wool roving Angelina Fibers
- self-leveling gel
- Stewart Gill Pearlise paint in Abalone
- FW ink in Pink Pearlescent

1. In your sketchbook, practice drawing stylized faces with a more realistic nose. Once you feel comfortable with your drawing, draw the face on paper and shade with pencils. The features don't have to be perfect, but you want a soft effect. Check your eye shading for harsh dark lines. Cut out the face and glue onto the canvas with matte medium. With pencil, sketch a simple body. Draw hair on the head and fairy wings on the body. Work from the sample on page 81 if desired.

2. With a palette knife, add fiber paste to your drawing. I have added it everywhere in this painting, but it is concentrated on the wings. It's hard to see the fibers in the paste when it's wet, but they show up when fully dry. To create even more texture, embed wool roving or Angelina Fibers into the wet paste on the wings. The fiber paste will look lumpy and funny but will be super fabulous when you spray on color later. Spread fiber paste and/or molding paste onto the hair and onto the background. Spread paste over a stencil to create words on the dress. Play with the pastes! Let everything dry overnight.

3. Spray the dried fiber paste with pink Radiant Rain (or use your own mix of acrylic paint and water in a spray bottle, in a color of your choice) and Chalkboard Glimmer Mist, and dab at parts with a paper towel to soften the color. Watch the magic! Dried paste begs for color and soaks it up nicely like a happy sponge. If the paint looks too dark, grab a water bottle and spray, spray, spray until it's lighter, letting it drip and do interesting things on the canvas. When the spray has dried, dab white paint straight from the tube onto the peaks of the texture to enhance them more. This is an easy process, but the end result looks complicated.

4. The paste on the hair gives the illusion of thick, coarse hair. I painted the hair with dark brown opaque paint straight from the bottle. Alternatively, you can spray watered-down Pearlise paint or FW ink onto the dried texture to get soft tones and contrast. Dry-brush a lighter color such as red onto the peaks to highlight. Use a stencil brush for this—it gets into the corners where regular brushes won't. Textures are also hard on brushes and will ruin good ones, so cheap stencil brushes are the way to go. Dab white paint onto the wings.

FINISHING

6. Keep laying down paint to build up depth. I used glaze mixed with magenta and violet around the figure to "lift" her away from the background. Paint her lips with a glaze of red and add pink glaze to the cheeks. Apply a dash of Polished Pigments mixed with gum arabic to both irises. Add glitter and sparkles. When you feel the painting is done, apply beeswax to the face. Use the iron to smooth it out. **Note:** Do not apply beeswax over the texturized areas; the wax will clump and look cloudy. If you feel the painting needs more of a finish, apply beeswax only over areas that are smooth (such as her torso). Or you can pour and spread out self-leveling gel, which will give it a glossy finish.

{ Tip }
Is your painting finished but you long for more texture? Add more thick mediums to create dimension and texture, as long as the area hasn't been beeswaxed.

5. Texture also comes to this painting from dried flowers. I've used paper and silk flowers, but there is no substitute for real nature. Brush matte medium onto the canvas, then place flowers. Lightly brush medium over the flowers to seal.

ANGEL

Contrasting the earthy fairy is the heavenly angel. Histori-cally, paintings made for the Catholic Church used gold leaf to imply divinity, so angels have more bling than fairies do. The emphasis is also on feathery wings (not real feathers—that could be corny) by using texture to imply them.

Objectives
- Making stylized features
- Using molding paste
- Stenciling

Materials
- graphite pencil and eraser
- Prismacolor pencils
- computer or thin drawing paper
- scissors
- matte medium
- 12" x 24" (30 x 61 cm) wood or canvas substrate (I used wood)
- palette knife
- molding paste
- Adirondack Color Wash spray ink in Lettucespray bottle
- paper towels
- paintbrushes
- Golden Fluid Acrylics in Jenkins Green, Pyrrole Red, Titan Buff, Interference Blue, Titanium White, and Quinacridone Redstencils
- beads, glitter, and sequins
- gold leaf
- beeswax or self-leveling gel
- Angelina Fibers
- quilting iron

2. Draw the body and wings on your substrate. With a palette knife, apply molding paste to the wings. Go over it several times, adding more paste. Make short and long sweeping strokes, to suggest feathers. Let dry overnight.

1. Just as with the fairy, make a soft face with a stylized nose. Cut it out and paste it onto your substrate.

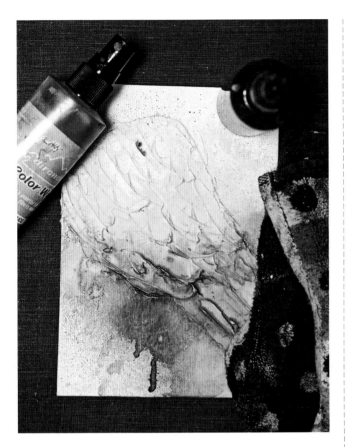

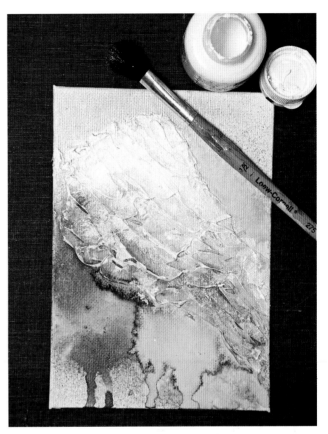

3. When dry, spray ink onto the wings and immediately spritz with clear water to dilute the color and create interesting drips. Blot with a paper towel to subtract color where it is too intense. I used a light green, a strange color for wings, but in the end you will just see it in the nooks and crannies. Green is the complement to red, the color that dominates this painting.

4. Dry-brush white paint over the wing peaks. Work the brush into the crevices at the top of the wings to imply form. Let more color show at the bottom. The green in the finished wings blends them into the rest of the painting. If they were only white, they would stand out too much.

5. Paint the dress Jenkins Green and the hair Pyrrole Red. Use Quinacridone Red for the darker hair around the neck. If you want the color even darker, mix a little green paint into the red. Use molding paste and a stencil to add flowers to the skirt. Let dry before dry-brushing with an accent color.

6. Stencil an angelic word at the bottom of the painting with molding paste. Adhere beads, glitter, and sequins to the word while it's still wet. Glue gold leaf around the wings. Add sequins and beads to the hair. Paint Interference Blue in areas of the dress and wings. To finish, coat with beeswax or self-leveling gel. (I used beeswax on the face and torso but left the textured wings alone.) Press Angelina Fibers into the wet leveling gel or hot beeswax, and lie flat until the wax or gel hardens. Smooth the wax with a quilting iron.

DESIGN TIP

Glitzy embellishments are used to enhance the figure, not upstage her. If, when you step back and look at your painting, you see more glitz than girl, dull down the bling with paint, or take some off. Sparkly things are fun, but too many take the focus away from the hard work you put into her face and the rest of the painting. Subtlety is key.

EXTRA CREDIT

So you have painted a beautiful girl, but what do you want her to say? As you did with your list of themes, images, and animals, make a list of words and phrases to use in your work.

Inspirational words: Trust, fly, sing, play, goddess, healing, strong, graceful, happy, imagine, explore, fabulous, glitter, grace, leap, bliss, sweet, wander, believe, hope.

Favorite quotations: Use quotations from your favorite book or fairy tale! My favorites:

"I say, if yer heart don't break once a day it shows a lack of imagination." –Lefty, *Prairie Home Companion*

"As a Woman, I have no country." –Virginia Woolf

For an alternative use for wings, create a winged heart for a journal cover.

PROJECT 5
La Sirena: Making a Mermaid Mosaic with Large Embellishments

If there is one thing I've learned in the four years I've taught online art classes, it's that we chicks dig mermaids. An overwhelming number of students requested this mermaid class–500 signed up in the first two months. I put off doing the class because I was never much interested in drawing girls with fins, but creating this workshop made me change my mind. Mermaids are lovely.

Whatever theme you choose to do, be it mermaids or Madame Butterfly, make it your own. Just because mermaids are traditionally ocean-dwelling creatures doesn't mean your painting has to have one. Mine doesn't. *Pez Puera Del Agua*, the name of this painting, translates to *Fish Out of Water* and reflects my mental state and physical situation when I painted this. I'd recently moved from the East Coast (New Jersey) to California (San Diego) and felt out of place. Everyone wore bicycle shorts and no one sounded like me. I lived skipping distance from Mexico and the color of the green and the way it meets the sky in the painting is how the border of Tijuana looked the day I saw it. I was also watching back-to-back episodes of the show *Weeds*, and although it wasn't planned, my mermaid reminds me of the main character Nancy Botwin with her flowing hair and red saucy fin.

ENCOURAGEMENT

You will get to a point in your work where your art will reflect your life. Be patient. Practice your skills and someday your mermaids might not have anything to do with the sea either. Let your imagination soar!

Objectives
- Incorporating large embellishments
- Cutting into wood
- Using glass bead gel
- Using heavy gel medium
- Using self-leveling gel

Materials
- graphite pencil and eraser
- Prismacolor pencils
- computer or thin drawing paper
- scissors
- matte medium
- 12" x 24" (30 x 60 cm) wood or 8" x 12" (20 x 30 cm) canvas substrate
- paintbrushes
- Golden Fluid Acrylics in Carbon Black, Pyrrole Red, Jenkins Green, Manganese Blue, and Titan Buff
- spray bottle
- paper towels
- carving knife
- leather gloves
- heavy gel medium
- scrap of decorative cloth
- Polished Pigments mixed with gum arabic in color of your choice (for eye color)
- beeswax in natural, blue, and green
- glass glitter
- mica chips
- mosaic tiles
- sequins
- bits of sea glass
- quilting iron
- gold leaf
- self-leveling gel

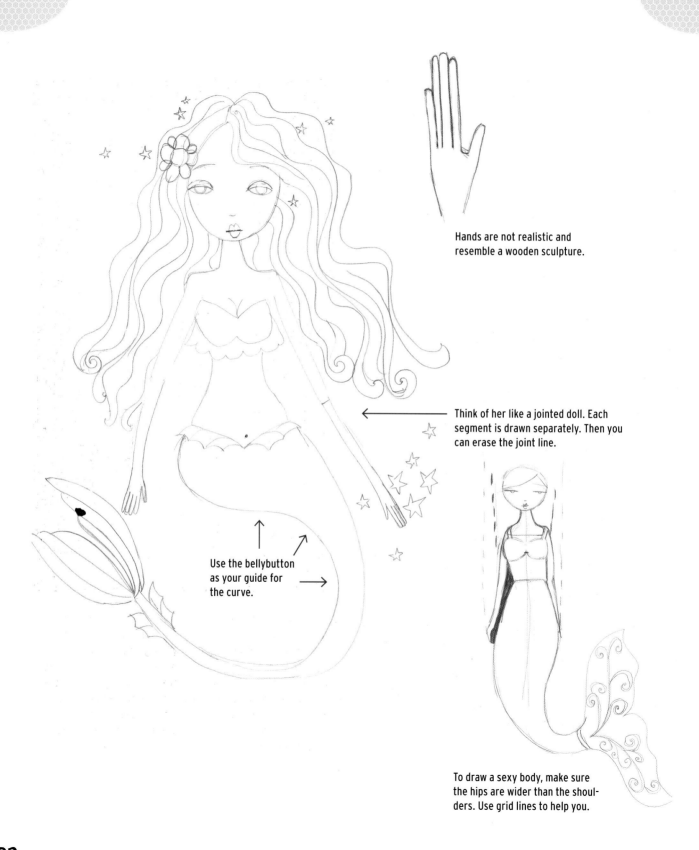

Hands are not realistic and resemble a wooden sculpture.

Think of her like a jointed doll. Each segment is drawn separately. Then you can erase the joint line.

Use the bellybutton as your guide for the curve.

To draw a sexy body, make sure the hips are wider than the shoulders. Use grid lines to help you.

1. Draw and shade a pretty face and glue her head onto wood with matte medium. Draw the body underneath her and in the background a horizon line to separate the earth or water from the sky. Draw with pencil a rough estimate of hair. Block in the hair and body with flat color. Because the figure takes up so much of the composition, there is not much background. Dab, spray, and blot paint around the figure to imply earth (or water) and sky, but don't cover the entire surface; let some of the wood show through.

2. Now here's what's new: I *love* carving into wood to create a distressed surface. My favorite tool is a curled blade wood-cutting tool, but anything sharp will do. I've often used a box cutter. Wearing leather gloves to protect your hands, slice, stab, and distress randomly around the painting. Carve in words. Take care not to hack into her pretty face. If you are using canvas, go easy with the carving. Your goal will be to lift the paint off the canvas, not cut the canvas.

4. Paint flowers and fish in the base color (shown here on a seperate canvas for clarity).

3. Spread heavy gel medium over the base-coated hair. Let dry overnight. To give more substance to the hair, paint over it with the same color or dab on a lighter color for highlights. Cut out a circle from the fabric to represent the sun and adhere it to the painting with matte medium. Spray or drip watered-down brown paint onto the painting and smear with a paper towel until it's as grungy as you like it. Paint eyes with Polished Pigments mixed with gum arabic so they pop. Lips are Pyrrole Red.

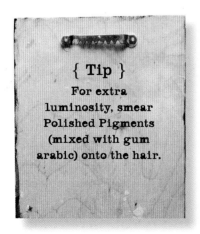

{ Tip }
For extra luminosity, smear Polished Pigments (mixed with gum arabic) onto the hair.

5. Drip natural beeswax onto the flowers and fish. Adhere glass glitter, mica chips, mosaic tiles, sequins, and/or sea glass in the beeswax. Iron the wax around the chips but keep the tops free and clean.

Finished chips in the painting.

6. Drip colored beeswax onto parts of the flowers: blue wax on blue flowers, green wax on green leaves. Glue gold leaf onto the tops of some of the mosaic chips.
If you put too many mosaic chips into the fin, the beeswax will clump and look cloudy. Drip colored beeswax over parts of the painting and over a few of the mosaic chips. Cut into the cooled wax to further distress the texture.

7. Finish off the rest of the painting, including her face, with self-leveling gel. I love how sparkly good glitter looks under the dried gel. Leave some areas of the wood bare with no finish to contrast with the shiny areas.

TRADITIONAL MERMAID

I've also made a more traditional mermaid in an ocean for you. As with all our mixed-media girls, start by drawing and shading the face and body, then adhere the girl to your substrate. These instructions are for creating a watery environment around her.

Materials

• graphite pencil and eraser
• Prismacolor pencils
• computer or thin drawing paper
• scissors
• matte medium
• 8" x 10" (20 x 25 cm) wood or canvas substrate
• blue and green spray inks
• spray bottle
• paper towels
• watercolor pencils
• ink pen
• rubber stamps
• blue StazOn ink
• glass bead gel
• heavy gel medium
• shells, pearls, mica chips, sea glass, and other shiny bits
• dry emptied teabags

1. Draw and shade a pretty mermaid and glue onto wood or canvas. Taking care to avoid the face, create a watery background by spraying the substrate with blue and green inks. Keep a spray bottle of clear water and paper towels nearby to wet the inks and blot off some of the color. Draw squiggles in the background with watercolor pencils or with an ink pen.

2. Randomly stamp over the background with blue StazOn ink. (The ink needs to be permanent so it doesn't wash off with more layering.)

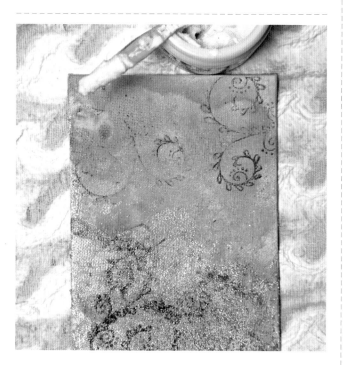

3. Spread glass bead gel over the blue-green background to give it an ocean feel.

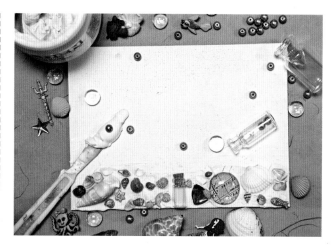

4. Spread heavy gel medium over the base of the painting to represent the sea bottom. Embed shells and pearly things into the gel.

5. Finish the mermaid with colors and embellishments of your choice. I used mica chips for the hair and dried, emptied teabags for her clothes.

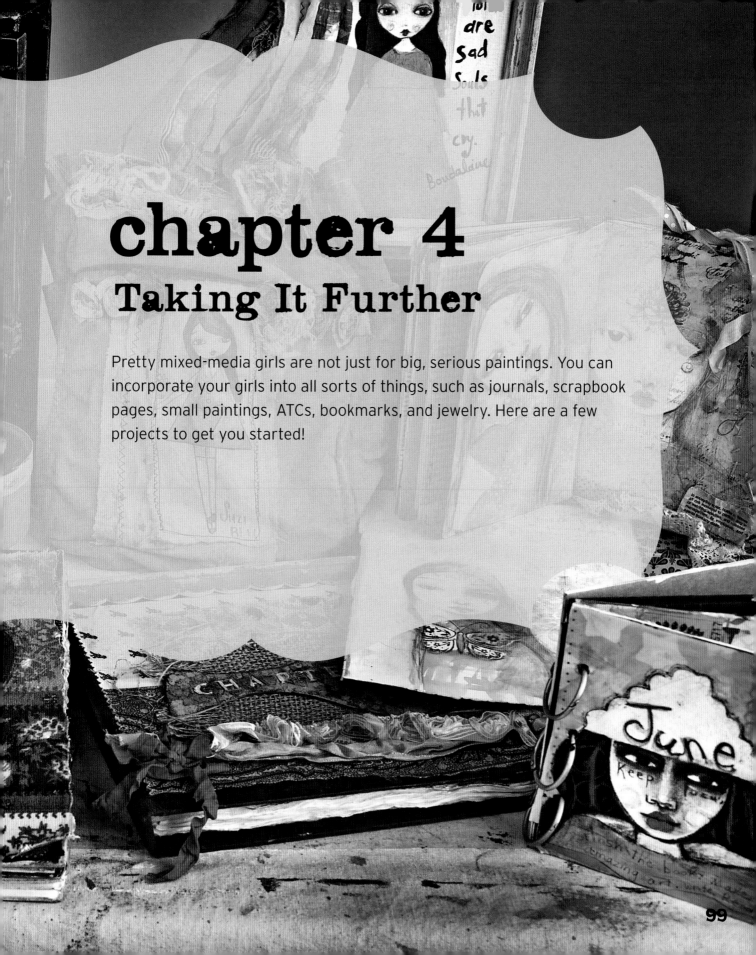

chapter 4
Taking It Further

Pretty mixed-media girls are not just for big, serious paintings. You can incorporate your girls into all sorts of things, such as journals, scrapbook pages, small paintings, ATCs, bookmarks, and jewelry. Here are a few projects to get you started!

Violins
are
Sad
Souls
that
cry.

Boudelaine

PROJECT 1
La Maison:
Houses for Your Girls

I like to think of frames as houses—an enclosed space for your pretty girl to live in. Adding a frame to a small painting is a cute way to finish it off and easy and inexpensive to do.

Materials
- canvas substrate
- frame to match substrate size
- gesso
- glazing medium
- paint
- wood molding
- tacky glue
- sandpaper

1. Make a painting on canvas board. Coat a cheap frame with a wash of gesso, then add color with a glaze of paint. Saw the molding to size and paint it to match the frame. Glue it onto the canvas with tacky glue. Sand the molding for a distressed look.

2. You can also glue decorative moldings straight onto the substrate to create the look of a frame without having one.

Artist } Margo Beatty

You can house your art in jewelry frames, making them a wearable showcase. With simple soldering, you can turn a high-quality print of your art into a pendant that everyone will see.

Artist } Elena Lai Etcheverry

Right: Think outside the box! No paint was used on this balsa wood box cover, just Prismacolor pencils.

PROJECT 2:
Scrapbooks and Journals

"I never travel without my diary. One should always have something sensational to read on the train."
—Oscar Wilde

As much as I desire to make art to put on walls, I love the idea of having my work close with me, in my purse, thrown on the table, next to my pillow at night: intimate, tangible, an ongoing story supported by words and photographs, sketches of the day. Painting girls inside journals is a way not only to practice your skills on a smaller scale but also to try out new things without the pressure that comes from hanging it on the wall for everyone to see.

My advice for keeping a journal you will love? Keep more than one. Your sketchbook is a place to practice drawings and ideas; your art journal is for paintings, good writing, moments of your life in photos. I will not work hard on a journal painting if in front of it is ten pages of outlined class ideas and stream-of-conscious complaining. Work on sloppy writing and ideas in a separate book and rip out the best pages for your journal. They can be painted over as a back layer or remain visible in a collage. Instead of being intimidated by the empty page, think of your journal as a place. Just like curling up with a book is a mini trip to places and events, opening your journal and working on it transports you to another world, one in which you can be anything and everything is possible. Work on the art inside your journal like it matters, but don't plan on showing it to anyone. You will, of course, because you'll love it and will want to share, but while you are making it, tell yourself it's for your eyes only. Because it is. When you create art with an eye to showing it to others, you become afraid to take chances. It's one thing to make a pretty page, but more compelling is something with depth that documents your real life. Whatever page you are doing, stay with it; don't be in a rush to get to the next.

Treat your art journal like you would a painting, remembering that the better the paper, the better your results will be. You can draw girls right on the page or on another page (like your sketchbook), cut them out, glue them down, and go from there. Layer just like you would on wood or canvas. You can even apply beeswax inside your journal!

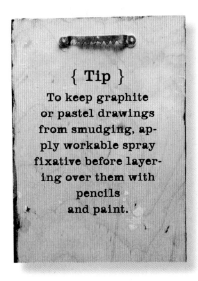

{ Tip }
To keep graphite or pastel drawings from smudging, apply workable spray fixative before layering over them with pencils and paint.

SCRAPBOOKING YOUR GIRLS

Cut out paper elements of things to decorate the pages: houses, crowns, doggies—it's your paper world!

Unlike a traditional art journal, scrapbooks are centered around photographs of memories we have had with people we want to remember. Take your photos further by drawing girls on paper, coloring and cutting them out, then gluing them down on the page. They don't have to really look like the people in the photographs—it's way more fun if they don't. Get the hair color and length similar and people will know who is who. Think of all the inspiration you will have by using family photos. La Petite Grandma, Le Petit Uncle Bob!

{ Tip }

Boys have square chins. And they wear pants. That is about the only difference I make when I draw them.

Want to bookmark the page where you left off in your journal? Draw girls onto cardstock and make them into pretty tags.

Draw and color your fur child onto cardstock and cut out. Put a Pop Dot behind it and attach it to the page.

DON'T FORGET THE FUR BABIES!

Lia Kent makes girls in her Moleskine journals.

Adhere girls to board book covers.

Pretty girls on fabric journals and tote bags.

It's not any fun to be only one. said Mitzie.

PROJECT 3:
ATCs and Mini Paintings

Is there a better handmade present than a mini painted canvas or an ATC? It's just large enough to be meaningful, and it won't take you forever to create. Little paintings can showcase a figure or illustrate a scene.

For this project, follow the same process and use the same materials as for the larger paintings (see chapters 1 and 2)—just make them smaller. For little paintings, I like using decorative papers with vintage patterns and colors. Notebook paper from composition notebooks works well for a childlike feel.

Materials

- graphite pencil and eraser
- Prismacolor pencils
- computer or thin drawing paper
- scissors
- matte medium
- small canvas or wood substrate (5" x 7" [12.5 x 18 cm] or smaller)
- decorative paper
- small paper punches: flowers, hearts, stars
- pages from old books
- paintbrushes
- Golden Fluid Acrylics in colors of your choice
- wood-carving tools
- glazing medium
- beeswax in natural, blue, and red
- quilting iron
- ribbons, buttons, tiny bows, rub-on words, rhinestones

A little fancy trimming adds interest to this simple painting.

1. Draw and shade a pretty head, and glue it to a canvas or wood substrate. Cut a simple folk art body from a piece of scrap decorative paper and glue that down as well. Add punched-out red hearts and text from old books. Paint hair, and when dry, cut into it with carving tools. Dig into the dress a little to shabbify that, too.

2. Mix brown paint and glazing medium and sweep around the figure to create a shadow and dirty everything up. Melt natural beeswax over the painting and iron smooth. Embed ribbons, buttons, and other ephemera into the hot wax. Drip a little blue wax on the front and red wax around the edges.

There is not much background to worry about in a little painting. It's a great way to use up scraps that you have in your studio.

Let some of the wood show through your little paintings. Scrape lines into the wax and fill in with brown oil paint. Wipe away the excess.

Be whimsical in your little paintings. Have fun with characters and what they are doing. Look through children's books for words and sentences that will explain your story.

LITTLE SYMBOLS

Hearts on clothing are everywhere in my art and symbolize loving or sorrowful emotions.

Every painting has a story to tell. What do your paintings say to you? Houses, cats, moons, stars: we are drawn to symbols for a reason. Look at the images in your work and make a list of symbols and what they mean to you in your sketchbook. They are *your* symbols and can be anything you want. Owls might be wise, but to you maybe they represent hunting (for knowledge or self-discovery). Having a list also gives you images to put in your paintings when you're stuck.

Here are some of mine:
- birds: freedom, or lack of it
- elephants: spirit, sacred life
- houses: feeling lost, wanting a home
- fish: emotional currents
- oceans: feeling overwhelmed
- wolves: boys who lie
- flowers: gifts
- party hats: celebrating life
- swirls: chaos

There's no place like home! Use Cloud Blue Prismacolor pencil for shadows around the little white dogs. Extras: red glitter for shoes, tiny license plate.

Ajae McCain used small pieces of wood to make ATCs (on left and right).

chapter 5
Student Gallery

I am including work that my students have done after taking my classes to show you that you too can learn to make pretty faces even if you have never drawn before, and once you get the hang of it, your style will be more your own. Even though we start out lining up the face the same way, there are an infinite number of ways to alter the face to make it different. I will critique each painting so you appreciate not only its beauty but also what makes it so successful.

I chose this painting by Mónica Mota to represent the classic Petite Doll: pretty and demure with a basic body shape and a simple background. Even though the composition is mostly just figure, subtle layering gives the work a more complicated look.

Mónica teaches us that a pretty face and a simple body are all that are needed to make a very lovely painting.

Artist } Mónica Mota

Letting Go by Sascalia

Artist } Ariane Reinhard

Ariane Reinhard has done stunning shading on these faces with colored pencils. Patterned paper breaks up the simple body shapes, and cutting into the wood adds design and drama.

Ariane teaches us to break up large areas of a simple body with patterned paper.

How darling is Sascalia's work? This is a very pretty girl in the middle of a heavily flowered background. Although this painting is not extremely layered, the tone of the background is soft and muted, giving it a retro feel. Flowers are cut out of paper and glued down. What could become very confusing is balanced to look at. This is because of the contrast between the soothing and muted background and the bright and vivid flowers (see the gypsy carnival painting for another example of this technique). There are no harsh lines in the painting. The tree trunks, flower stems, and limbs of the girl are curved and smooth, giving the painting a comforting and feminine feeling.

Sascalia teaches us to add scrapbook paper cutouts of objects for a whimsical feel.

Shattered by Joyce van der Lely

Quite different from Sascalia's painting is this haunting portrait by Joyce van der Lely. Although I did not go over the more complicated three-quarter face in this book, all of the techniques in this work are the same. The face is drawn with colored pencils and lightly tinted with glaze paints, which contrasts deeply against the heavily textured molding paste hair. Mosaic tiles were assembled to represent architecture, but they do not dominate the painting. And because the color palette is mostly monochromatic blues, there is no color to distract the viewer from the figure's soulful gaze.

Joyce teaches us to create a mood with careful use of color.

Artist } Angela Vedder

Angela Vedder made this painting for her daughter. Even if you don't sell your work or do not desire to be in galleries or teach art to others, you can practice your craft and make beautiful paintings for those around you to enjoy. Angela's daughter will always appreciate the time her mother took to make her something by hand. The colored pencil and glaze paint finish on this face is flawless and stands out against the background.

Angela teaches us to find inspiration in those we love.

Artist } Marianne VanWingerden

When adding heavy embellishments, pick one three-dimensional element and stick with it. Marianne VanWingerden used curled vintage music paper to make this painting come alive. If more objects were used in addition to the hair, like thick jewels and keys stuck in wax, it would look cheesy, but the artist had restraint with her sculptural element. The green butterflies add energy to the mostly cream palette, and the affirmation is one a viewer will want to read again and again.

Marianne teaches us to take risks.

Lily by Wendy Maynard

The gorgeous shading Wendy Maynard has done on the face and the rich color make this work compelling. Subtle layering of paper gives this work a complicated yet not overly noticeable texture. Her expression is deep but her blouse and whimsical hair and butterflies feel light and airy. I could look at this face forever.

Wendy teaches us that a great face doesn't need much going on around it.

Madam Butterfly by Rachelle Panagarry

Rachelle Panagarry has made an alluring girl with collage papers integrated into the face. The handmade paper the butterflies are made from give an organic feel as they feather out the sides.

Rachelle teaches us not to be afraid of layering.

Stay
True to You

Artist } Ajae McCain

Ajae McCain's style is all her own. Instead of introspective and pouty, this girl looks directly at the viewer as if to say, "I am here. I am not invisible." The trademark of Ajae's style is adding decorative paper for strands of hair and layering over them. Her palette is neutral and earthy and makes the figure appear down to earth.

Ajae teaches us to have faith that with practice we will develop our own style.

Artist } Ariana "Goog" Guarino

Two sweet angel friends hold hands. A 12" x 12" (30 x 30 cm) format is not as easy to work in as a rectangle format when making a single figure, so Googie has included two. Because the figures are symmetrical and centered, the scene is calm and balanced. Titan Buff-tinted tiles on the floor give the color an aged feel.

Goog teaches us that we can create a feeling of calm by using a symmetrical design.

Artist } Malin Walkeby

Malin Walkeby was one of the first students to take my portrait class, and although she came to me already knowing how to draw a face, whatever skills she learned from me helped her explode into her own magnificent style. The full and pouty lips and the incorporation of dreamy watercolor layers, bright colors, and realistically rendered bodies make Malin's work unique.

Malin teaches us to learn from teachers and then add yourself to your work.

Artist } Flor Larios

Flor uses small prints of her paintings to decorate a wooden bracelet.

Flor teaches us that we can use our girls over and over again to create new work.

templates

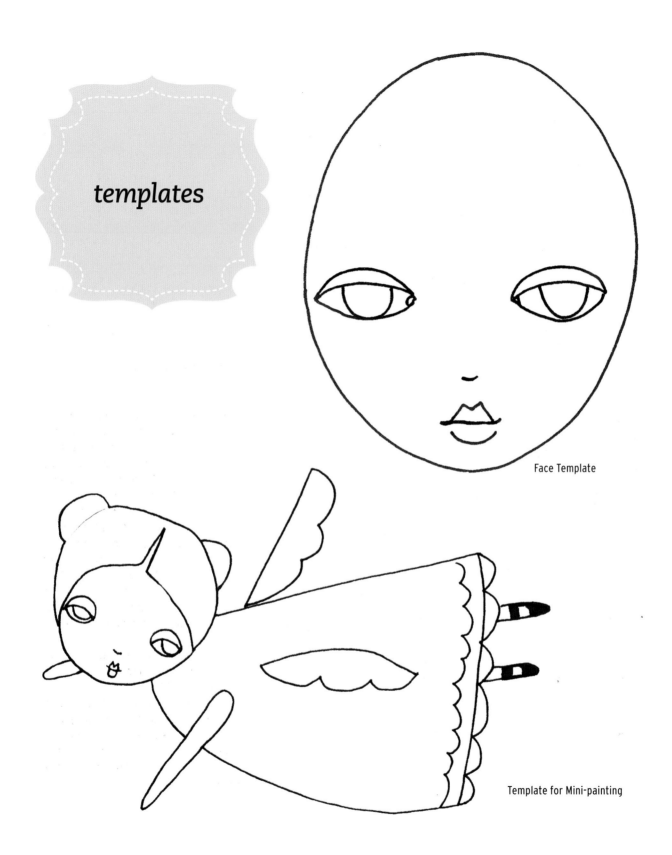

Face Template

Template for Mini-painting

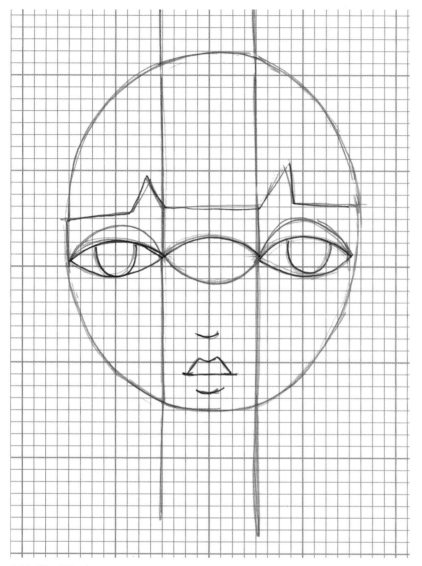

Grid without Numbers

GUIDELINES FOR USING THE TEMPLATES

Is it okay to use Suzi's templates to create paintings?

Yes! I want you to! Even if you know how to draw, when you shade and paint a face, you can change the look of it entirely.

Can I sell paintings I have made with Suzi's templates?

Yes, you may sell the original paintings you have made by using my templates as long as the art you made with my original template is not mass-marketed and sold to the world.

Can I submit paintings I've made with Suzi's templates to magazines?

You may submit paintings you have made with my templates to magazines such as *Somerset Studio*, but you must credit me with the drawing. Say, "This painting made with Suzi Blu Templates from the book *Mixed-Media Girls with Suzi Blu*." However, if everything is entirely your own, then you don't have to mention me at all; still, it would be nice if you could say you were inspired by this book. If I taught you how to do it, be super sweet and give me credit.

May I sell prints of paintings I have made with Suzi's templates (not my own drawings)?

No, you may not. To sell prints of your work, it must be 100 percent original and that includes the composition. If you traced my face template and used it in a painting, you cannot sell prints of that work.

contributing artists

Margo Beatty } www.margobeatty.com

Elena Lai Etcheverry, Charity Wings }
www.thetravelingprincess.blogspot.com www.charitywings.org

Brenda Figueroa } www.lafiorevida.blogspot.com

Ariana "Goog" Guarino } www.journeyofamermaid.blogspot.com

Lia Kent } www.artjunk.typepad.com

Flor Larios } www.florlarios.etsy.com www.florlarios.com

Wendy Maynard

Ajae McCain } www.ajaeunleashed.blogspot.com

Mónica da Costa Lobo Mota } www.mokicostalobomota.blogspot.com

Rachelle Panagarry } www.arteyecandy.com

Tascha Parkinson } www.tascha.etsy.com www.taschaparkinson.com

Ariane Reinhard } www.nara-studio.blogspot.com

Sascalia } www.sascalia.com

Joyce van der Lely } www.joycevanderlely-artist.blogspot.com

Marianne VanWingerden } www.ladybirdphoto.blogspot.com

Angela Vedder } www.attic2albums.blogspot.com

Malin Walkeby } www.mildamalin.blogg.se

resources

These are my favorite products. Tell them Suzi sent you!

www.alovelydream.com
For more Suzi class videos!

www.stampavie.com
Suzi Stamps

www.stewartgill.com
Creamy luscious paints. Alchemy Whirlwind is my favorite.

http://monamigabby.com
Fabulous foo foo trims

www.dickblick.com/products/prismacolor-colored-pencils
Prismacolor pencils

www.i-kandi.com/beeswax-encaustic-art-pigments.asp
Non-resin-colored and clear beeswax

www.clover-usa.com/products/268136/mini_irons
Clover mini iron

www.joggles.com
Dried pressed flowers

about the author

Known for her quirky videos and down-to-earth style, **Suzi Blu** is a leader in teaching art to women all over the world through her online school, Les Petites Academy. She lives in a gypsy cottage in New Jersey with her best friends, Gigi Rainbow Sparkle and Finney Foo Foo. She encourages everyone to be an artist.

dedication

I dedicate this book to Mickey, who was my father, but also my peer. I will deeply miss our conversations.
A mountain keeps an echo deep inside.
That's how I hold your voice.
—Rumi